THE NO GARLIC CC

This edition first published in July 2018

Printed and bound in the UK

ISBN: 978-1-9995948-3-1

A CIP catalogue record for this book is available from the British library.

This book can be ordered direct from the publishers at:

www.greentechpublishing.com

ACKNOWLEDGEMENTS

I would like to thank all the people who have acted as guinea pigs and consumed my delicious NON-GARLIC food over the years at all the fabulous parties that I have been honoured to host and serve. To my friends who are still here to tell the tale. To my late mother Betty, who unwittingly acted as the catalyst in developing my cooking skills, spurred on by her lack of culinary prowess, but who excelled in most other areas, including teaching me right from wrong as a child. Special thanks must also go to my daughters, who though their encouragement and love of my cooking over the years have motivated me to compile this book, the idea and inspiration of which has been sitting on the shelf for more than 10 years.

Finally, thanks go to the team at Greentech publishing who have provided the perfect balance of critical feedback and support, leading up to this book's first volume in what will be an ongoing series of NO GARLIC gastronomic scrumptiousness.

To all my friends and family who
after eating my food over many years,
are still here to tell the tale.

CONTENTS

 = SUITABLE FOR VEGETARIANS

THE NO GARLIC COOKBOOK
Let the flavour flood in

WELCOME

I want to show you how you can eat the most delicious meals without a hint of garlic in sight. All my recipes are incredibly satisfying and easy to cook.

Let me introduce you to a new way of thinking about how you cook food; one that I have developed and perfected over the last 20 years, in a way that is setting the trend in both the UK and Italy and is the de-facto protocol in Japan.

It involves eating the most mouth-watering and nourishing meals that are so familiar, without any need to add garlic or onion. It's a new way of cooking for most. The use of garlic in everyday meals is now so ingrained in our diet that even snacks like crisps can contain the dreaded G word. But to return to the concept of garlic free cooking, we have to go back to the 1960s, when the vast majority of meals were traditionally cooked with fresh wholesome ingredients and traditional spices and herbs.

I promise that you will find this book inspiring, to the extent that you will want to invite your friends and family around to taste your new full flavour garlic-free food, the way it used to be and the way it is now in most parts of Italy and the majority of Japan, as the tide against garlic is finally turning.

So, whether you have an intolerance or an allergic reaction to garlic, or you just want to go odour and garlic-breath free from now on, or are just inquisitive to know how great it could possibly be to eat garlic free. Then this book is for you.

INTRODUCTION

My relationship with food has always been a pleasant and rewarding experience, but garlic has been an unwelcome foe for as long as I can remember. I grew up in the cobbled terraces of inner Birmingham and every evening would retch and heave at the potent smell of garlic drifting from my neighbours' backyards at teatime. I didn't know then, but it was clearly my body warning me that this smell was not good for me. It was a form of bodily alarm.

In the sixties, garlic was not a mainstream ingredient in the typical British meal. The country was really only just getting over rationing from the war years and easy traditional meals tended to be the norm, made with what ingredients were available at the time. Thus, meals such as Sunday roast, fish and chips, bangers and mash, toad in the hole, and beans and cheese on toast, seemed to be the standard by which a growing family was nourished. Dessert was usually tinned sliced peaches with evaporated milk and a few slices of thin white bread and butter for afters. Apparently, bread and butter with dessert was a cheap way to fill hungry stomachs for the rest of the day.

Being a full-time stay at home mother looking after 4 children, her life was never easy. No washing machine, no fridge, no spin drier, no bathoom, just an outside toilet. Unfortunately for my Dad, brothers, sister and I, mums cooking was, to be blunt, below par. This was the catalyst that spurred me to develop my own cooking skills from an early age and is why I looked forward to school dinners so much.

Then about 15 years ago, I took a business colleague for lunch to a French Bistro. I remember vividly that the first course was pea and ham soup. Literally seconds after the first spoonful, I was told that my lips turned blue, I had difficulty breathing and then minutes later, stomach cramps commenced. This was the last time that I have knowingly eaten garlic and now make a point of thoroughly checking menus with waiters and chefs when eating out. Because of this problem, I can't eat processed food. Even snacks like crisps have the dreaded G in them. The upside is that all the food I eat, is prepared and cooked fresh, creating flavoursome culinary delights for all who eat with me.

THE HISTORY OF GARLIC

The plant, garlic, originated from Asia and is from the onion genus species. Its close family are chives, shallots, leeks and onions. It has been used by humans for many years for both medicinal and culinary purposes. Often used as a pungent flavour for spicy dishes. It is much paraded for its alleged super food traits and supposed health benefits. It has gained an almost cult like following amongst the likes of raw food fans, vegans and vegetarians. There have been many claims over the years that consumption can lower blood pressure, lower cholesterol and has antibacterial characteristics too. It has also been long known that some gardeners use it as a very effective organic pesticide, by placing it next to plants that need protection against pests or as a liquid spray. Due to the allicin chemical in each bulb, it is worth noting that there is no known animal that will eat this pungent vegetable. Of course, its taste and odour are enough to repel any potential predators, including vampires!

IS GARLIC A POISON?

Doctors recommend that pregnant women, especially those that intend to breastfeed, should avoid garlic completely as it has been linked to miscarriages as well as altering the behavioural patterns of infants (2). This alone should make one question its worth and safety for human consumption.

Garlic is a rubefacient matter and when directly applied to the skins surface in oil form, it will cause redness, swelling and often inflammation (1). This is the result of the immune system attempting to isolate the garlic so that it does no further harm to the body.

None the less, there are some assumed health benefits such as the ability to lower blood pressure (4) and its ability to lower cholesterol (3). It has been known for centuries that garlic is an anti-bacterial food that can totally destroy all bacteria, good and bad. Few people believe that that is a good thing though. Of course, most people want something that can kill off germs, but there can be destructive effects, worse even than having a bacterial infection, due to its nondiscrimatory characteristics. This is why I personally would not advocate consumption of garlic and there are even more reasons. Some studies have shown that garlic can cause damage to brain cells, due to its very powerful effect of entering the bloodstream, especially if eaten in raw form. Although, when cooked, the toxic or negative effect of garlic is greatly reduced.

Garlic can also burn. According to several sources, It has the ability to burn tiny holes though the lining of the intestines (2). This can be particularly bad for sufferers of IBS for instance. It can penetrate the mucus lining and proceed into the intestinal wall, burning tiny holes that can eventually lead to perforations and ultimately the garlic can then enter the bloodstream.

WW2 veterans, especially those of Italian descent, were extremely knowledgeable about the toxic effects of garlic. If you feed a dog raw garlic, you can kill it. Apparently, some frontline soldiers stocked up with garlic bulbs and after squashing a clove, covered the garlic fluid over their bullets and loaded their weapons. Anecdotal reports suggested that despite some pretty poor marksmen, the garlic laden bullets gave them an advantage when it came to killing their foe. The frontline Italian soldiers knew that once garlic entered the bloodstream, the enemy would die, wherever they hit them.

THE TIDE IS TURNING

Completely unrelated to the Italians wartime military tactics, there is a whole new movement in Italy that is moving away from adding garlic to food, especially when using fresh ingredients. There are many self-publicised 'garlic-free' restaurants appearing all over the country. A new renaissance where all the great chefs are learning to cook without garlic. I am very familiar with Milan, having worked there a few years ago. Even then, the vast majority of eateries
in this great Italian city, cooked garlic-free.

Interestingly, garlic only became popular in southern Mediterranean countries when there was a shortage of food and no fresh herbs or spices were available. This was particularly evident during war times. As poverty increased, fragrant spices were substituted for cheaper, widely available garlic to give their food some flavour. This trend spread thoughout the world during the major conflicts of the last centuries due to fresh food and spice shortages, affecting mainly the poor communities of each country. The trend of garlic reversal and eradication in Italy, will hopefully spread further afield.

It's no secret that a country, recognised as having some of the oldest residents in the world, has an almost completely garlic-free diet. The Japanese are very proud of their culinary traditions and they remain the only country in the world to gain UNESCO cultural heritage status for their food. It's no coincidence then that garlic is not a staple ingredient in any Japanese traditional food.

The recipe for Bolognese sauce in Bologna is fiercely protected by the local chamber of commerce and calls for absolutely no garlic in the recipe. Even the famous late great Italian chef, Marcella Hazan, insisted on no garlic in her tomato based dishes. She once said, 'the single greatest cause of failure in would-be Italian cooking, was the unbalanced use of garlic'.

The 'no garlic' trend of restaurants is slowly but surely evolving in the UK. I have a local restaurant that almost exclusively cooks the entire menu garlic free. Long may it continue. I long to see the day when the pungent, overpowering, foul smelling bulb, is eradicated from our shores.

In other words, the reason that there is an ensuing revolt against the use of garlic amongst some of the world's top chefs, is as Hazan puts it," real recipes don't lean on garlic as a crutch, because their ingredients taste better to begin with, they possess true flavour" ...Let the flavour flood in !

MY CHOICE OF RECIPES

I have purposely chosen a selection of my take on the most flavoursome, mouthwatering dishes from around the world. All garlic free, and none the worse for its absence. All meals have been tried, tweaked and tested on friends and family at numerous social events over the past 20 years or more.

There is one self-indulgent snack that I have slipped in by stealth, that has nothing to do with garlic. The ubiquitous Cornish cream tea; whose clotted cream is so unique that it has EU protected status. Not to be confused with any other cream tea, where the cream is often incorrectly put on the scone first.

Like me, many of you reading this book will have very busy lifestyles and so I have made the recipes as simple to prepare and cook as possible. If the recipe asks for mango chutney, I expect you to source a non-garlic jar from your local supermarket, rather than make your own. Making your own pizza dough is a must, but pastry for the Pasty – I use ready-made chilled pastry. But generally, almost all of the ingredients are fresh and readily available in your local stores.

BIBLIOGRAPHY

1. Baruchin AM et al. 2001. Garlic Burns p781-782.
2. Barnes J Anderson, Philipson JD. Herbal medicines. Pharmaceutical press, London. 2012.
3. Murray MT. The healing power of herbs. London. 4th edition. Original 1995.
4. Ackerman RT et al. Garlic shows promise for some cardo vascular risk factors. Arch intern Med. 2001:161: 813-824.

"

Thee nickels will get you on the subway, but garlic will get you a seat.

"

--- NEW YORK (JEWISH SAYING)

QUICK SNACKS & STARTERS

Traditional CHEESE & BACON TOASTED ENGLISH MUFFINS

Serves	4
Prep time	10m
Grill time	10m
Total time	20m

This mouth-wateringly tasty breakfast treat has always been a firm favourite with friends and family over the years. I first came across this great start to the day in a tiny bistro where I live, but alas, it's now closed. It is so quick and easy to make and so rewarding to eat. I hope you enjoy this delectable breakfast treat as much as I do.

INGREDIENTS

- 8 x fresh English muffins
- 250g (8 oz) of medium sliced back bacon
- 250g (8oz) of grated mature cheddar cheese
- 1 pinch of freshly ground black pepper
- 1 tsp of cayenne pepper

METHOD

1. Line your grill rack with alumium foil and lay the strips of bacon on top and grill on a medium heat until the rashers are crisp and golden brown – not burnt and then set aside.

2. Keeping the grill on a medium heat, now cut each muffin in half and place cut side up and place on to the foil of the grill rack. Next, put a handful of grated cheddar on each muffin, covering well. Now slice the bacon into roughly 50mm x 20mm strips, don't be too accurate! Add the bacon on top of the cheese and try to cover as much of the cheese, without doubling up on the bacon. Sprinkle a pinch of cayenne pepper to taste and then put under the grill for between 5 to 10 minutes, or until the cheese has bubbled and is golden brown. Serve immediately – hot and tasty

Milanese BASIL & TOMATO TOASTED THINS

Serves	4
Prep time	20m
Grill time	10m
Total time	30m

I often use this quick simple snack as a starter, a prelude to a tasty pasta, or as a mid-evening bite when thowing a buffet party. They are so crunchy and tasty and are best eaten after the baguette slices come out of the grill. The best and quickest way to toast the baguette slices is to use a sandwich toaster, because it cooks both sides at the same time. I first came across this tasty snack in the Italian city of Milan.

INGREDIENTS

- 1 x long, fresh French crusty baguette
- 6 large fresh sweet tomatoes
- 1 handful of fresh basil leaves
- 1 x tbsp of rock salt
- ¼ cup of virgin olive oil

METHOD

1. Wash, dry and take the leaves of the basil sprigs and coarsely chop. Then set aside.

2. In a small mixing bowl, add the olive oil, half of the basil and half of the salt. Then stir gently and set aside. Next, slice the tomatoes thinly and lay in staggered form on top of each other ready for adding later.

3. Slice the baguette loaf at a slight angle and make each slice quite thin, about 10mm (⅜"). Then lightly toast both sides until golden brown – not burnt. Once toasted, leave on a baking tray. On each mini toast, add a slice of tomato (should cover most of the toast), then sprinkle a twist of freshly ground rock salt over each tomato, add a light sprinkling of the remaining fresh basil on each completed toasty, then drizzle a tsp of the basil oil mix on the top and serve immediately. I have never had a negative response to these tasty bites. Hope you like them too.

Traditional **PRAWN COCKTAIL**

Serves	4
Prep time	10m
Chill time	2h
Total time	2h 10m

Don't be tempted to use shop bought Marie Rose sauce. Not only does it not taste as good as homemade sauce, but it almost certainly will have garlic in it. My take on the sauce is mouth-wateringly good. And its G free.

INGREDIENTS

MARIE ROSE SAUCE

- 2 tbsp of light mayonnaise
- 1 tsp of ground ginger
- ½ tsp of paprika
- 1 pinch of freshly ground black pepper
- 2 level tbsp of tomato ketchup
- Squirt of lemon juice to taste
- Small bottle of Tabasco sauce

FOR THE PRAWN COCKTAIL

- 500g (1lb) of fresh prawns
- 4 medium size sweet tomatoes
- 1 crispy cos lettuce
- 1 tsp of cayenne pepper
- 2 slices of buttered brown bread, sliced diagonally into 2 quarters per serving

METHOD

MARIE ROSE SAUCE

Using a medium size mixing bowl, add all the Marie Rose sauce ingredients and mix until thick, pink and creamy. Add lemon juice and Tabasco to taste. Cover and chill in the fridge for at least 2 hours.

PRAWN COCKTAIL

Wash lettuce thoroughly, shake dry and then slice in thin strips and set aside. Dice the tomatoes into small chunks about the size of your thumbnail and set aside. Wash the prawns under cold water, rinse well, then add the prawns to the bowl of chilled Marie Rose sauce and fold in thoroughly.

TO SERVE

Now using 4 wide cocktail or sundae glasses, layer the bottom of each glass with about a 75mm (3") layer of lettuce strips. Then add a heaped spoonful of the prawn sauce mix and spread across the lettuce without compressing it. Now add a few of the diced tomatoes and a dusting of cayenne pepper. It is best to chill the prawn cocktails for at least half an hour before serving. Serve with quarter slices of buttered fresh brown bread. Enjoy.

Marvellous MOZZARELLA WITH SWEET CHERRY TOMATOES

Serves	4
Prep time	20m
Total time	20m

This snack is visually great and tastes as good as it looks. This recipe is very simple, quick to prepare and my experience is that they usually disappear within minutes of placing on a serving dish.

INGREDIENTS

- 400g (1lb) of sweet cherry tomatoes
- 60g (2oz) buffalo mozzarella Cheese
- Freshly ground black pepper and sea salt
- Virgin olive oil or virgin rapeseed oil for dressing
- 4 lemon wedges

BASIL OIL

- A handful of fresh basil leaves
- 100ml (3½ fluid oz) of olive oil

METHOD

1. Place the mozzarella on a wooden chopping board and slice it fairly thinly.

2. Halve the cherry tomatoes and place them on plate.

3. For the basil oil, put the basil leaves in a processor, then pour warmed olive oil over the leaves. Add a pinch of salt and pepper to season and blend to a paste. Using a fine sieve, strain the paste though and set aside.

4. Place a few grains of the sea salt on top of each tomato half and trickle the basil oil over the cheese and tomato. Grind a little black pepper and serve.

Delicate CREAM CHEESE & SALMON CRACKERS

Serves	4
Prep time	10m
Total time	10m

Quick and easy to make and will always be appreciated by your guests.
Makes 16 simply delicious cracker snacks.

INGREDIENTS

- 110g (4oz) soft cream cheese
- 5ml (1 tsp) dried dill
- 5ml (1 tsp) of ground sea salt
- Freshly ground black pepper to taste
- 5ml (1 tsp) of lemon juice
- 90ml (3oz) of smoked fresh salmon slices
- 16 round crackers (your choice)

METHOD

1. Mix cream cheese, lemon juice, dill, salt and pepper until blended.
2. Spoon a teaspoonful of mixture on to each cracker.
3. Place a slice of the smoked salmon on top. Add ground black pepper to taste.

Homemade SWEET POTATO CRISPS

Serves	4
Prep time	10m
Oven time	2h
Total time	2h 10m

This treat has always been a firm favourite with friends. It is so easy to make and so delightfully healthy to snack on. I hope you enjoy these guilt-free crisps as much as I do.

INGREDIENTS

- 2 organic sweet potatoes - 150g (5¼ oz) each
- 30ml (2 tbsp) of olive oil
- Optional - 2 pinches of sea salt

METHOD

1. Position the baking rack centrally in the oven and Pre-heat to 120C (250F).

2. Thoroughly rinse and dry your sweet potatoes and slice them as thin as possible, using a crisp cutter or mandolin if possible, although a sharp knife will do. Just ensure that they are not too thick, as they won't crisp uniformly.

3. Add the oil to a mixing bowl and add the sweet potato slices, making sure both sides of each slice are coated. Add optional salt and gently toss the bowl to ensure even coverage.

4. Lay out a single layer of slices on a baking sheet and bake for about 2 hours, turning once, halfway though cooking, to ensure an even colour.

5. Remove the crisps once golden brown and brittle. It is important to let them rest to complete the crisping process. Serve when crisp.

Bonkers BANANA CRISPS

Serves 4

Prep time 10 m

Oven time 2-3h

Total time 3h 10m

Banana crisps really are the simplest of snacks to prepare and make. Just one ingredient aside from optional rock salt. They are visually stunning once cooked and are a big hit with all guests at any party.

INGREDIENTS

- 2 x fresh medium sized organic bananas
- 1 pinch of freshly ground rock salt - optional

METHOD

1. Position a rack centrally in your oven and place a baking tray, covered with a sheet of baking paper. Set the oven to 100C (210F).

2. Slice the two bananas in to 3-4mm thick slices (⅛") and lay on the baking sheet.

3. Bake until golden for 2 to 3 hours, turning each slice over half way though.

4. Leave to crisp and harden for at least 30 minutes at room temperature, then eat.

Creamy

CHEESE & HAM CARTWHEELS

Serves	4
Prep time	15m
Total time	15m

These cheese and ham cartwheels are made with delicious cream cheese spread, fresh slices of deli ham, rolled up on tortillas and cut into slices. The result is a fun starter or snack, great for any occasion. This is an ideal quick and easy appetiser! For more guests, just adjust the recipe to suit.

INGREDIENTS

- 1 x tortilla wrap
- Finely chopped sun-dried tomatoes
- 1 pinch of freshly ground black pepper
- 225g (8 oz) of plain cream cheese
- 60ml (¼ cup) of light mayonnaise
- Medium pack of thin deli style ham – 110g (¼lb)

METHOD

1. Combine cream cheese, mayonnaise, and sun-dried tomatoes in a mixing bowl. Mix until blended evenly.

2. Spread a thin layer of cream cheese mixture on your tortilla wrap taking care to spread it evenly so that the whole tortilla has a uniform thin layer.

3. Along the middle of the tortilla, place a few slices of deli ham to cover the width of the tortilla wrap. Place a layer of cheese on top of the ham to cover the width of the tortilla, ensuring that each cartwheel has cheese and ham.

4. Tightly roll up the tortilla wrap. Cut a small portion of each end off and discard, cutting the remaining tortilla roll into 6-8 slices, about 25mm (1") thick.

5. Either set aside and chill or serve immediately.

Gorgeous GOATS CHEESE, TOMATO & OLIVE TRIANGLES

Serves	2
Prep time	10 m
Total time	10 m

This mouth-wateringly tasty treat has been a summer favourite. It is really quick and easy to make and so delightful to eat. I hope you enjoy this tasty starter or snack as much as I do. For more guests, adjust recipe accordingly.

INGREDIENTS

- 4 x triangular slices from a wholemeal tortilla round.
- 50g (2 oz) of creamy goat's cheese
- 2 x 5cm (2") strips of cucumber, thinly sliced
- 3 sweet organic tomatoes sliced
- 4 black or green olives, coarsely chopped
- A handful of rocket leaves

METHOD

1. Cut 4 triangles of wholemeal tortilla rounds into large triangles
2. Now spread with the creamy goat's cheese.
3. Add the cucumber and tomato to top, add a few leaves of rocket and then sprinkle with olives. You can drizzle balsamic vinegar or dressing to taste.
4. Eat immediately.

Tasty TUNA LETTUCE WRAPS

Serves	8
Prep time	15m
Total time	15m

I use grated ginger to compliment the taste of mayonnaise. The lemon juice helps take away the fatty taste too. For the tuna wrap, using a chopped fresh tomato and green bell pepper strips, really adds texture to the tuna lettuce wrap. It's definitely a big hit in my home.

INGREDIENTS

- 180ml (6 oz) solid white canned tuna in brine
- 1 medium green bell pepper
- 1 x medium sweet organic tomato
- 1 pinch of freshly ground black pepper
- 1 tsp of cayenne pepper
- 1 wedge of lemon for juice
- 1 head of cos or romaine lettuce
- Dijon mustard
- 1 x 25mm (1") chunk of fresh ginger, finely grated
- 1 x 15ml (tbsp) of light mayonnaise
- Tsp of dried paprika

METHOD

1. Open and drain the tuna tin. Chop the bell pepper and grate the ginger.

2. Slice the tomatoes and cut out a wedge of lemon.

3. Combine the tuna, mayonnaise, mustard, paprika, ginger and black pepper in a mixing bowl.

4. Chop the bell pepper into small random chunks and stir together with the tuna mix.

5. Squeeze in juice from the lemon wedge and fold in.

6. Rinse and dry the lettuce and pull out the large leaves. You will need 8 of them for 4 people. Then spoon in about 125ml (½ cup) of the tuna salad into the lettuce. Wrap and enjoy!

Magnificent MAC & CHEESE

Serves	1
Prep time	10m
Microwave	6m
Total time	16m

There will be a chorus of despair ringing out across the land from professional chefs and cooks, at the very mention of a microwave in a serious cookery book. But that would be missing the whole point of this very quick, last minute, hot and tasty snack. We have all experienced a long gruelling day away from home, resisting the temptation of roadside cafes and their lukewarm, pre-prepared meals. This quick, easy and additive free snack, is a welcome break (excuse the pun) from the overprocessed on the go alternatives of motorway diners.

INGREDIENTS

- 80ml (⅓ cup) of macaroni pasta
- 60g (¼ cup) water
- 30ml (2 tbsp) semi skimmed milk
- 180ml (¾ cup) of mature grated cheddar cheese
- Pinch of salt and black pepper mix to taste

METHOD

1. Mix the pasta and water in a large mug and add the salt and pepper.

2. Put the mug mix into a microwave and cover with a loose laid paper towel. This prevents mess if it overspills during cooking. Cook on high for 2 minutes, then stop and stir.

3. Repeat this for 6 minutes, stopping and stirring at each 2 minute interval. The water will be thoroughly absorbed when the pasta is cooked though.

4. After 6 minutes of cooking, remove the mug and stir in the cheese and milk. Then microwave for a further minute. Stir the milk and cheese mix thoroughly into the pasta and eat immediately. Absolutely luscious.

NOTE: FOR MORE SERVINGS, JUST ADJUST THE RECIPE TO SUIT.

Zingy

CRAB SALAD

Serves   4

Prep time   40m

Total time   40m

This luscious tasty meal is lightly refreshing with delicate flavours. Crab salads are a fantastic idea for a summer lunch or afternoon snack. White and brown crab meat work well with this recipe, whether combined or used separately to augment the myriad of flavours and textures.

INGREDIENTS

CRAB MIXTURE

- 480g (1lb) of crab meat
- Zest of 1 lime
- Juice of 1 lime
- 30ml (2 tbsp) of virgin olive oil

CRAB BASE

- 50g (2oz) of (optional) finely chopped shallots (or 25mm piece of ginger –grated)
- 100g (4oz) of beetroot – diced
- 10g (½oz) of small radish, finely diced
- Rice wine vinegar

- 35g (1oz) of finely chopped apple with peel intact
- 25g (1oz) of crème fraiche
- Freshly ground black pepper
- Sea salt

GARNISH

- Crisp cos or romaine lettuce
- 1 avocado chopped
- Handful of thin sliced radish.

METHOD

1. For the crab mix. Place the shallots (or ginger) over a low heat in a pan and just cover with rice wine. Cook until shallots (or ginger) are clear and soft. Do not burn. Then take off the hob and allow to cool to room temperature

2. Add the cooled shallots (or ginger) with the beetroot, radish, apple, crème fraiche and salt and pepper into a separate mixing bowl and fold until evenly mixed. Set aside.

3. Check crab meat for any bone or pieces of shell, then fold in the mix with the remaining zest of lime, juice of lime and olive oil, taking care not to break down the crab flakes too much. Add salt and pepper to taste. Then chill in the fridge.

4. As an option to scattering the crab meat over the salad, you can serve the meat mix, by placing a mould ring in the middle of each plate. Add 25g (1oz) of the crab base mix to each mould, then top with 65g (2½oz) of the crab meat. Garnish with Cos lettuce leaves, avocado and sliced radish. Serve immediately.

Super SALMON SUSHI ROLLS

Serves	6
Prep time	20m
Rice prep	45m
Total time	1h 5m

Salmon is one of the most common ingredients in sashimi, nigiri, rolls, and other raw sushi dishes. Eating fish raw always carries some amount of risk, so preparing the salmon properly is key. You should start with fresh, high-quality fish, but cleaning your work area and tools is also important to avoid the spread of bacteria. If you choose whole salmon for your sushi, you'll have to cut and debone the fish properly too. I prefer to get my fishmonger to fillet a new fish in front of me and slice it there.

INGREDIENTS

- 150g (6oz) Fresh sushi grade fillet of salmon
- 4 slices of smoked salmon
- 1 x ripe avocado
- 150g (6oz) of mascarpone (Italian cream cheese)

- 600g (2½ cups) of cooked sushi rice (follow manufacturer's instructions)
- Small pack of nori (seaweed paper)

FOR THE SIDE

- Small saucer of good quality Japanese soy sauce as a dip

METHOD

1. Place the rice on the nori, using 150g of the cooked sushi rice. Do not compress the rice.

2. Place cling film on the rice, flip over the nori and rice. Then add the filling on the empty side of the nori sheet. The filling consists of fresh salmon strips, avocado strips and mascarpone cream cheese.

3. Using a sushi mat, roll the sushi mix.

4. Now cover the top of the roll with the Smoked Salmon.

5. Wrap in cling film to retain the mix and fish, then cut into slices about 25mm (1") wide, using a saw-like action, to prevent the roll being compressed and flattened. Lay on a white plate (for best effect) and serve with soy sauce.

NB: The use of a sushi mat will be a huge help now and in the future.

Fresh # SALMON SASHIMI

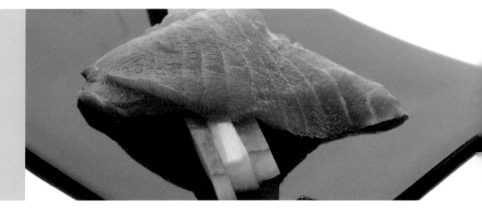

Serves	6
Prep time	5m
Total time	5m

In the past few years I have learnt to really appreciate Japanese food. Even more so after my trip to Japan in 2017, where I learnt that Japanese food is an art form, so much more than most people who live abroad perceive it to be. I love sashimi and I had a lot of it in Japan! Favourites of mine are salmon and tuna based. As it is really hard to find sushi/sashimi grade tuna in the west generally, I present this, salmon sashimi. You can serve the salmon sashimi with plain soy sauce. Simply dip a slice in a small bowl of good quality Japanese soy sauce, then eat immediately.

Just like the previous Japanese appetiser, sushi, salmon sashimi is absolutely delightful, healthy, nutritious and very low in calories as it is mainly protein with essential fatty oils. Once tasted, you will always crave for this dish. Because we are not in Japan to witness and taste their culinary delights, this is the next best thing. Just make sure you buy your fish fresh on the day you make it. Have fun!

INGREDIENTS

- 450g (1lb) Fresh sushi grade fillet of salmon

FOR THE SIDE

- Small saucer of quality Japanese soy sauce as a dip

METHOD

1. The browner meat on salmon is not used for sashimi. All we need is pure flesh. Trim any excess off.

2. Now cut the fish up into little slices that are about 16mm (½") thick. A sharp knife is essential, so take care!

3. Lay the slices of salmon sashimi on a plate in a circular pattern with the edge of each one on top of the other. Now enjoy with your Soy dip.

Awesome AVOCADO WITH PRAWNS & CRAB

Serves	6
Prep time	20m
Total time	20m

This is a great snack, especially if time is not on your side. Easy to prepare and readily available ingredients. It makes for the perfect accompaniment to any main course.

INGREDIENTS

- 3 ripe avocados
- 170g (8 oz) of crab meat (tinned or fresh)
- 250ml (Cup) of light mayonnaise
- 1 pinch of freshly ground black pepper
- 30ml (1 tbsp) of lemon juice
- 15ml (1 tbsp) dried cayenne pepper
- 15ml (1 tbsp) dried paprika
- 12 large cooked king prawns
- 15ml (1 tbsp of tomato ketchup/sauce)

METHOD

1. Cut avocados in half and gently remove the stones. Thinly slice and set aside.

2. Drain the crab meat and place in a mixing bowl.

3. Try to avoid breaking up the crab meat too much. Fold in the mayonnaise, lemon juice, paprika, prawns and tomato ketchup/sauce.

4. Next, divide the crab mix equally to each plate and dress the sliced avocado either side of the crab meat mix. You can add thinly sliced strips of bell peppers and thinly sliced boiled egg to top off, to add to the presentation.

5. Serve immediately or set aside and chill.

Cornish CREAM TEA

Serves 4

Prep time 15m

Total time 15m

This is a quintessentially traditional English afternoon tea, originating from Cornwall. There is nothing quite like sitting down with scones, jam and cream and a nice refreshing cup of English breakfast tea blend with a drop of milk. Delicious.

INGREDIENTS

- 8 all butter scones – plain or fruit
- 125g (3½ oz) of quality Cornish clotted cream
- 60g (2oz) of good strawberry or raspberry jam preserve
- Pot of English breakfast tea – for 4 people

METHOD

1. Take the scones and halve them horizontally.
2. Lay out on a chopping board, cut side up and spread a thin layer of the jam preserve on each scone.
3. Now add an equal dollop of Cornish clotted cream to each scone. It is important to note that this is the Cornish method and for some unknown reason it simply tastes better than with the cream first.
4. Pour tea for 4 and enjoy the most indulgent and tasty afternoon snack ever.

"

Jam first or clotted cream first?
Jam first at Buckingham palace
parties!

"

--- FORMER ROYAL CHEF. DARREN MCGRADY

MAIN COURSES

BEEF

Scrumptious BEEF FILLET STIR FRY

Serves	4
Prep time	15m
Hob time	10m
Total time	25m

I first experienced this mouth-watering dish in a teppanyaki restaurant in China. The fillet beef was so tender and tasty with a compliment of flash fried fresh veg. It is such a healthy, nutritious meal, yet so quick and easy to make. I hope you enjoy it.

INGREDIENTS

- 450g (1lb) of fresh beef fillet steak – cut into strips
- 2 tbsp of rapeseed or vegetable oil
- 125g (4½ oz) of broccoli florets
- 2 carrots, sliced thinly
- 1 pinch of freshly ground black pepper
- 1 red bell pepper, sliced into thin strips
- 1 chopped spring onion
- 25mm (1") of fresh ginger, finely grated
- 2 tbsp of toasted sesame seeds
- 1 tbsp of good quality soy sauce

METHOD

1. Take a large frying pan or wok and heat the oil over a medium to high heat until browned (about 3 minutes). Set aside the fillet beef strips

2. Add broccoli, red pepper, carrots, ginger and spring onion to the pan and stir fry for about a minute.

3. Add beef and now stir all ingredients for a further minute. Add a tbsp of soy sauce and the sesame seeds and cook for a further 1 minute. Now serve immediately on to pre-warmed plates and enjoy.

Succulent CORNISH PASTY

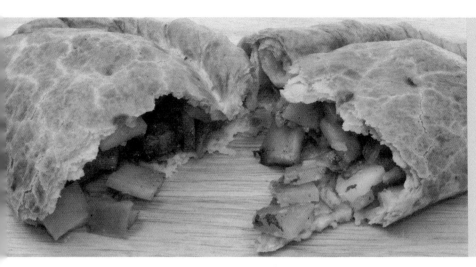

Serves	4
Prep time	20m
Oven time	1h
Total time	1h 20m

This mouth-wateringly tasty traditional Cornish pasty has always been a firm favourite with friends and family over the years. It is so simple and easy to make, especially using pre-made chilled pastry and so rewarding to eat. I hope you enjoy this delectable whole meal in one as much as I do.

INGREDIENTS

- 450g (1lb) of quality beef skirt, cut into 20mm (¾")
- 450g (1lb) of potato, diced
- 250g (8oz) of swede, diced
- 200g (½lb) of sliced onion (optional)
- Salt and white pepper to season
- 1 beaten egg to glaze the pastry
- 2 blocks of 500g chilled ready-made shortcrust pastry

METHOD

1. 1. Pre-heat your oven to 165C (310F)
2. Take the pastry blocks from the fridge and leave to reach room temperature for about 30 minutes.
3. Roll out each block of pastry on a work surface lightly dusted with flour. Using a round plate (approximately 20cm or 8" in diameter), cut out 4 circles of pastry.
4. Layer the vegetables and then place an equal amount of meat on the top layer of each pasty. Add plenty of salt and white pepper over each layer that you build in at a ratio of about 2:1.
5. Now fold over the top of the pastry circle on each pasty and starting at one end, crimp the pasty along the bottom of the case (not the top, as this will then become a Devon pasty!). Glaze with the beaten egg using a baking brush.
6. Pierce small hole. Bake at 165C (310F) for 55 to 60 minutes until golden brown.

Juicy

FILLET BEEF, WILD MUSHROOM & PARMA HAM

Serves	6
Prep time	30m
Oven time	45m
Total time	1h 15m

This fantastic main course is without doubt amongst family and friend's favourites. It does take a little time to prepare, but believe me, it is worth the wait. Cooking the fillet beef in a cocoon of Parma ham and mushroom filling, makes for the most tasty, moist and flavoursome steak that you could imagine. Paired with my vegetable recommendation, you cannot fail to impress your guests.

INGREDIENTS

- 1 kg (2.2lb) trimmed fillet of beef
- 1 grated 50mm (2") chunk of fresh ginger
- 50g (2oz) unsalted butter
- 28g (1oz) dried wild mushrooms or porcini
- 10 large slices Parma ham or prosciutto

- 5 sprigs of fresh thyme
- ½ a lemon
- Rapeseed oil or olive oil
- 4 sprigs of fresh rosemary
- 250ml (1 cup) drinkable red wine (if it tastes bad cold, it will taste bad hot!)

Serve with roast potatoes and steamed greens on the side.

METHOD

1. Preheat the oven to 220°C (425°F) and position rack centrally.

2. Allow meat to get to room temperature for at least 30 minutes prior to cooking.

3. Fill a mixing jug with 500ml (pint) of boiling water and add the dried wild mushrooms. After about 20 minutes, drain and set aside.

4. Place a large frying pan over a high heat with 1 knob of butter. Add the wild mushrooms, grated ginger and 2 tbsp of water, then reduce the heat to low and simmer for 5 minutes, or until thick and syrupy.

5. Squeeze in the lemon juice and stir in the remaining butter, then season to taste with the pepper and sea salt. Leave to cool for a few minutes.

6. Drizzle 1 tbsp of oil over the beef and season with black pepper. Seal in a roasting tray over a medium heat on the hob until browned all over, then take off the heat.

7. Place the slices of Parma ham out on a large piece of non-stick baking paper so that they're just overlapping and big enough to wrap around the beef. Spread the hydrated mushrooms lengthways over the centre half of the prosciutto, then place the fillet of beef on top.

8. Now carefully roll up the meat and filling. Detach the paper and gather the ends of the Parma ham. Secure and tie with butcher's string.

9. Place in the oven and cook for 25 minutes for rare, 35 minutes for medium, or 45 minutes for well done. Once the meat has been cooking long enough for your choice of tenderness, place the meat on a chopping board to rest for 5 minutes, pouring any remaining juices back into the tray.

10. Now, heat the tray over a medium to high setting on the hob, add the wine and simmer to your desired thickness.

11. Remove from the hob, then pour the juices though a sieve before serving. Let the meat rest for at least 20 minutes before serving.

12. Carve the fillet roll and serve. Lightly pour over the red wine sauce.

Delicious CHILLI CON CARNE

Serves	4
Prep time	50m
Hob time	30m
Total time	1h 20m

This chilli con carne is without doubt, the ultimate version that I have perfected over the years. Simple to cook and mouth-wateringly tasty this main course has always been a firm favourite amongst friends. It is so quick and easy to make and so rewarding to eat. I hope you enjoy this low to medium hot chilli. For a hotter chilli, just add more chilli powder to taste.

INGREDIENTS

- 1 tbsp of oil
- 1 red bell pepper
- 25mm (1") fresh grated ginger
- (optional) 1 medium onion, diced small
- 1 tsp of Ground cumin
- 1 tsp Paprika
- 500g (1lb 2oz) of lean minced/ground beef

- 380g (1lb) can of chopped tomatoes
- 1 beef stock cube
- 2 level tsp of medium chilli powder
- 1 tsp of dried marjoram
- 1 tsp of palm sugar or caster sugar
- 2 tsp of tomato puree

- 1 380g (1lb) can of well rinsed kidney beans
- Half a cup of drinkable red wine (optional)
- 2 cups of long grain rice, boiled as pack, to serve
- Soured cream to serve as a side dish.

METHOD

1. Prepare the vegetables. Chop the optional onion, diced into small chunks, or grate the fresh ginger. Cut the red pepper into thin long strips, discard the seeds.

2. Put a large frying pan on a medium heat and add the oil. It should be hot and ready to fry in about 1 to 1½ minutes. Now add the onions and cook until they become transparent and soft. Now add the red pepper, ginger, chilli powder, Paprika and ground cumin. Stir together for about 5 minutes. Set aside in the pan.

3. Now in a separate frying pan, add a tbsp of olive oil and leave for a minute or so on a high heat. Now add the mince/ground meat and as you stir, make sure you break up the meat so that it isn't in clumps, but is broken down into individual beads of meat. Keep stirring and breaking down for about 7 minutes. Fry on hot until the meat turns a nice golden brown. Turn heat down to simmer.

4. To make the chilli sauce, crumble the beef stock cube into 300ml (10 fl oz) of hot water. Now pour this into the beef pan. Pour in the can of tomatoes and stir. Next, add the marjoram and sugar, add salt and pepper to taste (2:1 ratio) and stir. Now squeeze in the tomato puree and stir on simmer for about 5 minutes.

5. Add the other pan of vegetables and spices, together with the meat and bring to the boil. Then immediately turn the heat down, simmer and cover with the lid, mixing occasionally. If necessary, add a few tbsp of water to the sauce if it looks like it's drying out. It should start to look moist, juicy and thick.

6. Rinse the kidney beans thoroughly, drain and then add to the mix, gently stirring them evenly in the pan. At this stage, taste the chilli sauce and if it needs more chilli powder add another tsp of dried chilli until satisfied with the strength. Cook for a further 10 minutes on low heat.

7. Now leave to stand for 15 minutes with the lid on. This is an important part of the process and it enables all the flavours to permeate though the mixture.

8. Now serve with the sour cream and rice.

Juicy

ITALIAN MEATBALLS IN A RICH TOMATO SAUCE

Serves	4
Prep time	20m
Cook time	2h
Total time	2h 20m

This is a very easy and delicious recipe. Homemade meatballs are much nicer than shop bought and the same goes for the tomato sauce too. You can make double the amount and refrigerate half for later in the week. In fact, the second half always seem to taste so much better after leaving the meatballs to marinate in the rich sauce over a few days in the fridge.

INGREDIENTS

FOR THE MEATBALLS

- 500g (1lb) of lean minced/ground beef
- 25mm (1") of fresh ginger - grated
- 1 cup fresh breadcrumbs
- 1 tsp of grated parmesan cheese
- 1 tbsp of dried parsley
- 1 tsp of ground black pepper
- ½ tsp of oregano
- 1 tbsp of olive oil
- 1 egg, beaten

FOR THE SAUCE

- 1 500g (1 pint) of tomato passata
- 1 crumbly chicken stock cube
- ½ cup of drinkable red wine
- 1 chopped and fried mild shallot (optional)
- ½ tsp of dried basil
- Salt and ground pepper to taste
- ½ tsp of brown or demerara sugar
- ½ tsp of oregano

METHOD

1. In a large mixing bowl, blend the beef, breadcrumbs, parmesan cheese, parsley, oregano, and black pepper. Mix with your hands until all ingredients are combined. Roll out into small balls about 30mm (1¼") in diameter. Now set aside on a greaseproof paper lined baking tray.

2. In a large saucepan, add the olive oil and fry the shallot (if using) until soft and transparent, not burnt. Now stir in the wine and simmer for 1 minute to ensure that most of the alcohol evaporates.

3. While on a medium heat, add the tomatoes, crumble the stock cube in the mix, add the oregano, the sugar and the basil. Simmer for half an hour.

4. Now add a tbsp of olive oil in the frying pan and on a high heat, fry the meatballs in batches until each meatball is lightly browned all over. You may need to do this in 2 or 3 batches.

5. Next, add the meatballs to the sauce, bring to the boil, then immediately lower the heat to simmer for a further 1½ hours. Place the lid on the saucepan, stirring gently every 10-15 minutes.

6. Now serve, either with pasta, spaghetti or on its own, with a sprinkling of grated parmesan and ground black pepper to taste.

Brilliant BEEF BOURGUIGNON

Serves	6
Prep time	45m
Cook time	3h 30m
Total time	4h 15m

My first recollection of eating this gorgeous wine and beef-based meal was in Normandy on a day trip in my teens. The memory of its mouth-watering taste and crumbling beef has stayed with me ever more. After several years of experimenting with many ingredients, this recipe has proved to be the best and closest to the original French recipe, minus the garlic. Like me, I hope your memory of this rich, hearty, beef meal stays with you for life.

INGREDIENTS

- 1.5 kg (3.3 lb) of braising steak
- 2 bottles of red wine
- 2 tbsp of rapeseed or olive oil
- 1 pinch of freshly ground black pepper
- 4 bay leaves
- 50mm (2") chunk of fresh ginger, grated

- Bunch of fresh parsley, washed and chopped
- A small bunch of fresh thyme
- Optional. 8 peeled shallots left whole
- 2 tbsp of tomato purée
- 8 medium carrots peeled and chopped into large chunks

- 3 tbsp of plain flour
- 450g (1lb) of baby mushrooms, washed and whole
- 300g of bacon lardons
- A large knob of butter

METHOD

1. Put the beef into a large mixing bowl and add the wine, a pinch of salt and pepper, thyme, ginger and bay leaves. Cover tight with plastic film and leave in your fridge overnight.

2. Next day. Pre-heat the oven to 200C (400F). Strain the marinade and beef into another bowl, reserving the wine and set aside.

3. Heat a tbsp of the oil in a pan on high heat in a large frying pan. Brown the meat in batches and set aside. Now using the same pan, pour a little of the wine in to the pan and stir, releasing any caramelised remnants from the beef browning. Transfer to a bowl and set aside.

4. Next, heat the rest of the oil in the large empty frying pan on a medium heat and gently fry the carrots and optional shallots, until they start to lightly brown. Stir in the flour for about a minute, then add the tomato purée. Next, add the beef, remaining juices, rest of the herbs and the wine. Season, bring to the boil, then immediately simmer, stirring all the time. Transfer into a casserole dish and cover.

5. After about 2 hours of oven cooking, heat the butter in a frying pan, add the bacon and fry for about 10 minutes on a medium heat until the bacon becomes crispy. Add and stir into the beef bourguignon and carry on cooking as above for a further 20 to 30 minutes.

6. Serve straight from the oven and sprinkle with the chopped parsley on the top of each serving.

Hearty # BEEF STEW

Serves	4
Prep time	20m
Hob time	2h
Total time	2h 20m

This is a quick and easy to make simple but tantalisingly tasty beef stew that never fails to amaze. This is a real warming hearty meal, especially in the winter months. The red wine adds a richness to the stew like no other. You can also try the same amount of good ale as a substitute.

INGREDIENTS

- 400g (14oz) of stewing steak, cut into 25mm (1") cubes
- 2 medium peeled and 25mm (1") cubed potatoes
- 1 tbsp of rapeseed or vegetable oil
- 2 beef stock cubes
- 1 tsp dried parsley
- 1 small onion (optional)
- 25mm (1") chunk of freshly grated ginger
- ½ litre (16 fl oz) of water
- 100ml of good red wine
- 1 tsp of cornflour
- 2 carrots cut into small chunks
- 2 celery sticks chopped into small slices
- 1 tsp of dried rosemary
- ½ tsp of ground black pepper

METHOD

1. Take a large saucepan with lid. Heat the oil and fry beef on a medium heat on the hob, until lightly brown.

2. Dissolve stock cubes in ½ litre of boiled water, mix and then pour into the pot over the beef cubes. Stir in the pepper, parsley and rosemary. Now stir in the red wine. Bring to the boil and reduce the heat to simmer for 1 hour.

3. Now stir in the carrots, (optional onion), celery and ginger into the pan and then dissolve the cornflour in 2 tsp of cold water. Mix into paste and stir in the stew. Simmer and cover for a further hour. Serve with fresh crusty bread.

"

I am a great eater of beef, and
I believe that does harm to
my wit

"

--- WILLIAM SHAKESPEARE

CHICKEN

Tangy CHICKEN BALTI CURRY

Serves	8
Prep time	45m
Cook time	2h
Total time	2h 45m

Originating from the Pakistani quarter in Birmingham UK, during the 1960's. This is without doubt, my most popular dish amongst friends and testament to this supremely tasty aromatic dish, rarely is any left for the next day. This is a simple, but unequivocally rewarding meal. It is simple to make. I prefer to marinade the chicken, the day before. The longer the chicken infuses, the tastier it becomes. This is the fruitiest, tangiest curry loaded with aromatic meat that just melts in your mouth and tastes so good. There is of course no pungent garlic to mask the true fragrant flavours of this mouth-watering Balti curry.

Perfect for any season, the secret of this tasty dish is to plan in advance to ensure adequate time is given to let the marinating process do its job properly.

INGREDIENTS

- 900g (2lb) of skinned and boned chicken thighs
- 25mm (1") of fresh ginger - grated
- 4 x 400ml (14floz) cans of chopped tomatoes
- 2 jars of no garlic mango chutney
- 4 tbsp of garem masala
- ½ a cup of red wine
- 1 tbsp of ground cumin

- 3 sprigs of fresh coriander
- 3 tbsp of green cardamom seeds
- 1 tsp of sea salt
- 100ml (4oz) of red wine
- 1 x chicken stock cube
- 100g (4oz) of fresh Greek yoghurt
- 8 plain naan breads (bought locally)

- 1 whole chopped red pepper
- 1 handful of plain sundried tomatoes
- 10 sliced shitake mushrooms
- A few glugs of olive oil or rapeseed oil

FOR THE MARINADE

- Small 200g (8oz) of fresh Greek style yoghurt
- 25mm (1") of fresh ginger - grated
- 1 tbsp of garem masala
- 1 tsp of turmeric
- 1 tsp of sea salt

METHOD

1. Mix all the ingredients of the marinade mix and stir by hand. Add in the chopped chicken thighs. Cover with plastic film and pop in the fridge. Ideally, leave overnight or for at least 30-40 minutes before continuing with the recipe.

2. Using a large saucepan, add the olive oil over a high heat on the hob.

3. When the oil is sizzling, add the ginger and green cardamom seeds and fry on a medium heat, turning ingredients over for about 3 minutes.

4. Now add the wine and heat for about 3 minutes, stirring regularly until reduced by a third.

5. Add and crumble the chicken stock cube into the wine mix and stir in thoroughly.

6. Now add the tins of chopped tomatoes and mango chutney and bring to the boil, stirring constantly, then immediately simmer on a low heat.

7. Add the sea salt, sun dried tomatoes, red pepper, shitake mushrooms, garem masala and ground cumin. Stir in and bring to the boil. Then simmer on a low heat.

8. Next, add the marinated chicken thighs and bring to the boil. Then immediately lower heat and simmer for 1½ hours, stirring occasionally.

9. Add the Greek yoghurt, bring to the boil, then serve in Balti dishes immediately.

10. Add fresh coriander leaves to garnish. Serve with hot naan bread. Enjoy

Aromatic THAI GREEN CHICKEN CURRY

Serves	4
Prep time	30m
Hob time	30-40m
Total time	60-70m

This fragrant Thai green curry is without doubt, a really popular dish amongst guests and family. This is a supremely tasty aromatic curry, rarely is any left for the next day, but once cooled can be refrigerated and used within thee days of making it or frozen for up to a month. This is a simple, but hugely rewarding meal. It is so easy to make if you pre-prepare my green curry paste found on page 54. This is the tastiest non-garlic Thai curry that my guests have ever savoured. I hope you feel the same way too.

INGREDIENTS

- 1 tbsp of rapeseed oil or vegetable oil
- 2 tbsp of my green curry paste (page 54)
- 8 chicken thighs, boneless and cut into chunky strips
- 2 tbsp of Thai fish sauce
- 3 lime leaves

- 1 tbsp of palm sugar or caster sugar
- Freshly ground black pepper and ground sea salt
- A handful of trimmed and rinsed green beans

SERVE WITH:

- Fragrant Thai rice. Cook to packet instructions
- Optional chopped fresh coriander leaves to dress on rice

METHOD

1. Heat the oil in a large frying pan or wok until it just starts smoking. Add the Thai green curry paste and stir fry until it bubbles – about 1-2 minutes.

2. Now add the chicken strips and gently stir until coated in the paste and fry for a further 1 minute. Do not over-fry until brown because this will toughen up the chicken. I prefer eating it tender and melt in the mouth.

3. Add the coconut milk, fish sauce, palm sugar and lime leaves, stirring continuously until it starts to boil. Now reduce the heat to simmering and continue for a further 8-10 minutes, making sure you stir the mixture gently thoughout until the liquid has thickened.

4. Now add the green beans and continue to simmer for 2-3 minutes, regularly stirring, until the beans are just tender. Add ground pepper and salt to taste.

5. Make the rice.

6. I normally spoon the rice into a ramakin and gently pack down. Then tip over and empty the moulded rice onto a large bowl. Then spoon or ladle the Thai green curry over the rice, scatter the lime leaves over and eat.

Fragrant GREEN CURRY PASTE

Makes 200g (7oz)

Prep time   20m

Hob time   20m

Total time   40m

This is a base paste that can be used in a whole host of curries, but in particular, it is the key ingredient for my Thai green curry on the previous page. It is medium hot, but the chilli content can be lowered for a milder version or added to make it hotter, depending on your preference.

INGREDIENTS

- 25g (1oz) of cumin seeds
- 50g (2oz) dried coriander
- 25g (1oz) of coriander seed
- 1 tsp of dried nutmeg
- Optional – 10 mild shallots
- Handful of fresh basil leaves
- Handful of coriander leaves
- 1 tbsp of Thai fish sauce
- 75mm (3") of freshly grated ginger

- 10 medium sized green chillies
- 5 lemongrass stalks, with outer leaves removed and then finely chopped
- 50g (2oz) of shimp paste
- 1 tbsp of lime juice

METHOD

1. Add the dried coriander, nutmeg and cumin seeds to a dry frying pan over a medium heat. Dry fry until the seeds start to colour and release their fragrant aromas. Now remove from the heat then grind with a blender or in a spice mill.

2. Add the peeled shallots (if using) in a blender, then add the coriander leaf, chillies, lemongrass, shimp paste, basil, lime juice, ground spices and Thai fish sauce. Now blend to a smooth paste. This paste is now ready to use, batch and store. It is worth making a large batch and to freeze the unused paste for up to 2 months. For convenience, place paste in ice cube trays. You can use it straight from the freezer.

Succulent SLOW ROAST CHICKEN

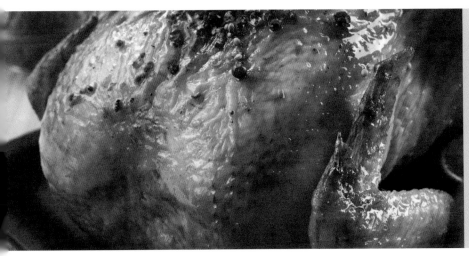

Serves	4
Prep time	15m
Cook time	4h
Total time	4h 15m

This mouth-wateringly tasty slow roast chicken treat, once prepared, can be left cooking on a low heat while you spend time with your guests or family. When you pair this chicken, with my crunchy roast potatoes and roasted vegetables, it never fails to delight family and guests alike. The chicken just melts in your mouth and that's the way all good meat should be. I hope you enjoy this delectable main course as much as I do.

INGREDIENTS

- 1.8kg (4lb) whole corn fed free range chicken
- 1 tbsp of butter
- 4 sticks of celery
- 1 tsp of dry marjoram
- 1 pinch of freshly ground black pepper
- 1 tsp of dried parsley
- 1 cup of drinkable red wine
- 1 whole lemon, washed and slit
- 1 tbsp of rough ground rock salt

METHOD

1. Pre heat your oven to 120C (250F). Mix the parsley, marjoram and ground black pepper in a mixing bowl until combined. Now add the red wine and stir together. Add to mix into roasting tin and set aside. Make sure that the chicken has no retaining string left in place.

2. Now melt the butter and brush all over the chicken, including the crevices between the legs and wings. Next, lightly scatter the rock salt over the chicken.

3. Place in the pre-heated oven until the meat is no longer pink and juices run clear. You can extend cooking time to 5 hours if necessary. Remove chicken from the tin, cover with foil and allow to rest for 15 minutes before serving.

Scintillating **COQ AU VIN**

Serves	4
Prep time	20m
Cook time	1h 20m
Total time	1h 40m

This French classic has been transformed into a garlic free delight for me and the truth is, nobody has ever mentioned the absence of garlic; only the great lingering taste and tender 'fall off the bone' chicken. Don't ever be tempted to use chicken breast as the braised thighs and chicken legs will provide much more flavour. I hope you enjoy this delectable meal as much as I do.

INGREDIENTS

- 6 complete chicken thighs, with skin and bone
- 6 chicken legs on the bone with skin
- 250g (8 oz) of bacon lardons
- 2 tsp of plain flour
- 2 tsp of butter

- Half a full bottle of red wine
- 5 sprigs of fresh thyme
- 250g (9oz) of chicken stock
- Pinch of course sea salt and ground black pepper
- 20 rinsed and dried button mushrooms

- Optional – 6 small mild shallots
- 1 50mm (2") piece of fresh grated ginger

METHOD

1. Pre-heat the oven to 200C (400F)

2. Season the chicken thighs and legs with salt and black pepper.

3. Place the bacon in a frying pan and cook over a medium heat until lightly browned. Set aside the bacon on a few sheets of kitchen paper.

4. Leave the remains of the frying pan and add the chicken thighs and legs, skin side down. Fry until lightly browned. Set aside the chicken to a plate.

5. Lower the heat, low to medium and add the mushrooms and optional shallots. Sauté until golden brown.

6. Now stir in the flour and butter until completely combined.

7. Transfer the contents of the pan into a flame proof casserole dish and on a low heat, pour the red wine into the dish and stir the bacon and thyme into the red wine mix. Simmer until the wine is reduced by about a third. Now add the chicken stock to the mix and add the chicken, bringing to a simmer, just gently bubbling.

8. Now put the casserole in the pre-heated oven for 30 minutes. Occasionally spoon the juices over the chicken and continue cooking for a further 30 minutes or longer until the chicken is no longer pink and the juices run clear.

9. Now transfer the chicken to a warm serving bowl.

10. Transfer the juices of the casserole dish into a saucepan over a high heat and reduce the liquid, until the sauce thickens, skimming any settled fat off the surface. Season with salt and pepper, remove the thyme and pour the sauce over the chicken. Optionally, serve with fresh vegetables and mashed potato.

The Perfect SUNDAY ROAST CHICKEN

Serves	6

CHICKEN

Prep time	15m
Cook time	4h
Total time	4h 15m

I can promise you that this will be the most mouth-wateringly tasty Sunday roast that you have ever eaten. Crunchy roast potatoes, delightfully crispy roast vegetables mated with tender fall off the bone roast chicken. It has always been much-loved by friends and family, not just for Sundays, but as a hearty mid-week winter warmer too. I hope you enjoy this delectable Sunday roast as much as my friends, family and I do.

INGREDIENTS

- Roast chicken (Page 55)
- Roast vegetable bake (Page 81)
- Crispy roast potatoes (Page 80)

METHOD

1. Using the following recipes in this book, follow the instructions, combine together and serve for the most amazing Sunday roast ever. Enjoy.

   a. Crispy roast potatoes – page 80
   b. Roast vegetable bake – page 81
   c. Slow roast chicken – page 55

POTATOES

Prep time   15m

Oven time   55m

Total time   1h 10m

VEG

Prep time   15m

Oven time   45m

Total time   1h

LAMB

Luscious MOROCCAN LAMB TAGINE

Serves	4
Prep time	30m
Cook time	2h 30m
Total time	3h

This fragrant, authentic Moroccan lamb tagine will be well worth the pre-preparation and slow cooking. I have narrowed it down to 7 simple steps. I prefer to use premixed dried spices called Ras el Hanout (literally – top of the shop' in Arabic), perfect for any tagine and used by all good Moroccan chefs thoughout their country.

Ras el Hanout is widely available in good supermarkets and consists of: coriander, ginger, smoked paprika, allspice, cardamom, mace, nutmeg, turmeric, cayenne pepper, saffron and rose petals. The aroma of this spice mix is amazing! This meal is a firm favourite and never ceases to attract praise when served and eaten. I hope you enjoy this luscious meal as much as I do. It's well worth the wait!

INGREDIENTS

- 2 tbsp of ground black pepper
- 1 kg (2lb 2oz) of shoulder of lamb, cut into 50mm (2") chunks
- 600ml (1 pint) of tomato passata
- 2 tbsp of olive oil
- 1 pinch of freshly ground black pepper
- 4 mild shallot onions, diced in to very small diced cubes (optional)
- 1 tbsp of dried parsley
- 120g (4oz) of dried apricots
- 55g (2oz) dates
- 2 400g (1½ pints) of chopped tomatoes
- 85g (3oz) flaked almonds
- 600ml (1 pint) lamb or chicken stock (non-garlic)
- 2 tbsp of good quality clear honey
- 1½ tbsp of Ras el Hanout

METHOD

THE NIGHT BEFORE YOU COOK.

Place the lamb into a medium sized bowl and add 1 tbsp of Ras el Hanout spice mix. Now add the chunks of lamb into the mix, gently toss the meat and fold in so that every piece of meat is covered with the spice mix. Cover with plastic film, put in the fridge and leave overnight.

THE NEXT DAY.

1. Preheat the oven to 150C (300F)

2. Put a frying pan on a high heat and add the olive oil. After a minute or so, add the onion (if using) and cook until it is transparent and soft in texture. Take out, clean pan and set aside.

3. Now using the same pan, add oil and heat again for about a minute on high. Add the marinated lamb chunks and fry until all the chunks of lamb are browned, but not burnt. Add the meat and onion into a casserole dish. Now using the goodness left in the frying pan, add about 600ml (1 pint) of the lamb or chicken stock and stir, scraping up all the fragrant spices left on the pan

4. Now add these juices to the casserole dish.

5. Add the tomato passata, apricots, dates, ½ tbsp of Ras el Hanout spice mix and honey into the casserole mix. Bring to the boil, add the lid and then oven cook for 2 to 2½ hours until the meat is 'falling apart' tender.

6. Place the tagine in a pre-warmed serving bowl or tagine and sprinkle over some chopped parsley. Enjoy!

PIZZA & PASTA

Ultimate PIZZA NEAPOLITAN

Makes 4, 12" pizzas

Prep time   20m

Prove time   1h 15m

Cook time   10m

Total time   1h 45m

TOPPING:

Prep time   15m

Total time   15m

This is without doubt the ultimate pizza base recipe. I first made this dough about 15 years ago, after experimenting with various different recipes. It is best made with stone ground bread flour. This recipe is really simple and can be made thick or thin. I prefer thin and crispy, like the authentic Southern Italian pizza. For this recipe, I have used a base Margherita style and added a few additional toppings to make a truly scrumptious feast. It is important to make the base sauce from fresh, providing an explosion of mouth-watering flavours. Perfect for any time of the year.

INGREDIENTS

INGREDIENTS FOR DOUGH BASE

- 1 cup of warm water (about 15C)
- 2 tsp of active dried yeast
- ½ tsp of granulated sugar
- 1 tsp of table salt
- 2 tsp of olive oil
- 750ml (3 x cups) of stone ground flour

INGREDIENTS FOR TOPPING

- 2 tsp of dried basil
- 250g (I cup) of pitted black olives
- A handful of sun-dried tomatoes (non-garlic)
- A pinch of fresh ground black pepper
- 250g (½ lb) of grated mozzarella cheese

- 2 tsp of dried oregano
- A handful of fresh basil leaves on each pizza
- Optional: jalapeno peppers

METHOD

BASE TOMATO SAUCE TOPPING

1. Pour the tomato passata into a mixing bowl
2. Add 1 tsp of dried oregano
3. Add pinch of salt
4. Add 2 tsp of dried basil
5. Now mix thoroughly and set aside.

> TIPS: Always gently stir and soak the dried yeast for about 5 minutes in warm water. For a crispy crust, lightly brush olive oil around the edges of the pizza base, before putting it in the oven. Always bake on the highest heat – preferably 250C (450F) to 300C (550F) or the ovens maximum temperature.

PIZZA DOUGH BASE

1. Measure water in a measuring cup, then add the dried yeast and sugar. Stir gently then leave to stand until it is foamy and active – about 5 minutes.

2. By Hand: add salt, oil and two cups of flour into a large steel mixing bowl, stirring in the yeast mixture using a large metal spoon. Add the third cup of flour and mix and fold the dough thoroughly until it becomes difficult to mix. Then, with your hands, work the dough into a large ball. It should be slightly sticky at this stage.

3. Now spray or apply olive oil with a paper towel to the inside of a second mixing bowl and then add your pizza dough. Brush a thin film of olive oil on the top of the dough. Cover the bowl with a tight layer of plastic film. Place in a warm area of the kitchen or I prefer to leave it in the airing cupboard for between 1½ to 2 hours, dependant on ambient temperature. The dough is ready to use when it has doubled in size.

4. When the dough is ready, empty the dough onto a lightly floured work top or large wooden board. Knead the dough ball vigorously for about 5 minutes, then cut the dough into 4 equal parts, forming dough balls and leave to stand for about 15 minutes.

5. Now flatten and stretch each dough ball to your desired thickness and diameter ready for topping. Don't worry about getting the perfect circle. I prefer the look of odd shaped pizzas to give the rustic look of real homemade cooking.

6. Put two baking or pizza trays into the hot oven to preheat – 250C (450F) – 300C (550F), putting baking parchment paper on top of each tray.

7. Add the tomato base sauce adding the other ingredients. Top off with the grated mozzarella cheese and complete with draped sliced prosciutto ham. Use two teaspoons of oregano equally and lightly sprinkling over the whole of each pizza. Add olives, ham and jalapenos as required.

8. OPTIONAL: for crusty edges, lightly brush the crust with olive oil

9. Now place onto the parchment in the pre-heated baking trays and cook for between 15 – 20 minutes on 250C (450F) or for 10-15 minutes for 300C (550F).

10. The pizza is cooked once the cheese is melted and the crust is light brown.

Authentic TAGLIATELLE ALLA BOLOGNESE

Serves	4
Prep time	30m
Hob time	3h
Total time	3h 30m

After carrying out a long drawn out investigation and research, on October 17, 1982, the Bolognese chapter of the Accademia Italiana della Cucina, announced this recipe as the official method to create true Bolognese sauce. Although I am certain that each Italian family will have their own recipe. I found this authentic method a few years ago and have since found that no variation betters it. Best of all, like so many truly authentic Italian recipes, there is no garlic to be seen! You can add a small amount of optional onion for added authentic flavour. If onion is out of bounds, substitute it for the ginger option.

In Italy, Bolognese sauce is rarely served with spaghetti since it tends to slip off the pasta and remain on the plate. In its place, the people of Bologna traditionally serve their celebrated meat sauce with tagliatelle.

Genuine Bolognese contains no tomato sauce, but I have added a handful of sun dried tomatoes that adds an additional layer of flavour and trace of sweetness to what is a complex fusion of flavours. Bolognese is epitomised by its long, slow cooking. In this case, it starts with simmering the meat in milk (to lower any sharpness of the sun-dried tomatoes added later) and red wine.

INGREDIENTS

FOR THE SAUCE

- 200g (10½ oz) of good quality ground/minced beef
- 100g (5oz) of good quality ground/minced pork
- 150g (5oz) pancetta - unsmoked
- 50g (2oz) onion – minced (or use ginger below)
- 50g (2oz) ginger – minced (instead of onion above)

- 50g (2oz) celery – minced or finely diced
- 50g (2oz) carrot – minced or finely diced
- ½ glass of drinkable red wine (if it tastes bad, don't use it!)
- 30g (1oz) concentrated tomato puree/paste
- 180ml (¾ cup) of fresh semi-skimmed or whole milk

- 28g (1oz) Porcini mushrooms (dried)
- Handful of sun dried tomatoes
- Olive oil
- Sea salt and pepper

ADDITION

- 150g (5oz) fresh tagliatelle
- Sea salt to flavour

METHOD

1. Fry the pancetta lightly in a few tsp of olive oil until its fat starts to seep out. Do not over-fry.

2. Add the vegetables and fry, stirring occasionally until the onions are transparent.

3. Now add the beef and pork mince until it is lightly browned, ensuring there are no clumps of meat.

4. Add the tomato puree/paste.

5. Now add the milk, drop by drop, until it is absorbed completely

6. Season with ground black pepper and sea salt.

7. Cover and cook for 3 hours so that the sauce simmers, stirring very occasionally. Add milk if it starts to look dry.

8. Serve with freshly cooked tagliatelle (don't succumb to serving with spaghetti)

9. You can toss the pasta with a knob of butter and then add a touch of grated parmesan cheese before adding to the delicious sauce.

Crispy RAGU PASTA BAKE

Serves	4
Prep time	45m
Cook time	30m
Total time	1h 15m

This mouth-wateringly tasty pasta bake is always a firm favourite with friends and family. It is so quick and easy to make and so scrumptious to eat. I hope you enjoy this delectable meal as much as I do.

INGREDIENTS

- 450g (1lb) of lean mince/ground beef
- 2 tbsp of olive oil
- 1 pinch of freshly ground black pepper
- 1 finely chopped carrot
- 1 finely chopped celery stick
- 3 bay leaves

- ½ cup of dry roasted breadcrumbs
- 25mm (1") ginger or 1 optional finely chopped mild shallot
- Cup of red wine
- 2 400g (12oz) tins of chopped Italian tomatoes

- 250g (9oz) of pasta shells or tubes
- 250g (9oz) grated mozzarella
- 1 tsp of dried oregano
- A sprig of basil leaves chopped roughly

METHOD

1. Heat a large frying pan and add oil. Brown the meat on a high heat for 8-10 minutes. Now transfer on a side plate and set aside. Add another tbsp of olive oil on a medium heat and fry the onions, celery and carrot until soft and transparent but not browned. Season with salt and pepper to flavour.

2. Now add the bay leaves and stir gently in with the cooked meat. Now add the red wine and let it simmer and gently bubble for a few minutes, then pour in the tomatoes and simmer for about 20-25 minutes with the lid on the pan, stirring every 5 minutes.

3. Now heat the oven to 200C (400F) and then fill a saucepan large enough to take all the pasta, with hot water. Add a tsp of ground sea salt and bring to the boil. Now cook the pasta for a further 3 minutes only.

4. Drain pasta and arrange the tubes or shells in a large 2L (½ gallon) baking dish and then ladle on the sauce, ensuring that all the tubes or shells are filled. Next, sprinkle the grated mozzarella over the top and be quite generous with the amount that you use.

5. Now mix the breadcrumbs and oregano with a tbsp of olive oil and then evenly scatter the mix over the pasta and cheese topping. Finish off with a liberal coating of parmesan cheese. Bake for 25 minutes or when it's a lovely golden crispy finish. Sprinkle basil leaves on top and serve immediately.

PORK

Succulent SLOW COOKED STICKY PORK BELLY

Serves	6
Prep time	10m
Oven time	4h
Total time	4h 10m

This is my signature sticky slow cooked pork belly. It is such a simple, but utterly rewarding meal and is so easy to make. I prefer to roast in the oven in a cast iron casserole dish, for aromatic meat that just falls off the bones and it smells so good. Best of all, there is no pungent garlic to mask the true flavours.

Perfect for a summer barbecue or as a hearty meal to warm you up in the midst of winter. The secret of this dish is to simply thow the pork slices in a pot, add the mix and cook slowly, you will never fail to get gorgeous tender meat.

You can never tire of making or eating these delicious pork belly strips. Perfect for all the family and full of nutritious goodness. This meal has all the features of a perfect tasty feast: slow cooked, easy and delectable — I have never had anybody utter a bad word about this meal. Serve on a bed of mashed potato topped with fresh, sweated spinach, drizzled with the juices from the meat pot.

INGREDIENTS

- 1 Kilo (3lb) of pork belly, each slice cut in half
- 25mm (1") of fresh Ginger - grated
- ¼ cup oyster sauce
- ¼ cup honey
- 2 tbsp cooking wine (Rice)
- Juice from two limes
- 2 handfuls of baby leaf spinach
- Mashed potato

METHOD

1. Cut each pork rib from large rack. Place pork ribs in the pot or casserole dish. Mix the remaining ingredients together and pour over the ribs.

2. Slow cook on 140C (280F) for 4 hours.

3. I much prefer homemade mash using either Maris Piper or a good red skinned fluffy potato. Topped with sweated spinach, made in a frying pan with just a knob of butter for no more than 1 minute. Place the ribs on the mash and spinach and drizzle with the pan juices. Serve hot.

I use a cast iron casserole dish, but you can use a slow cooker, the meat should be soft within 4 hours of slow cooking, making a supremely tasty melt in the mouth meal for 6.

Crispy PORK BELLY, SWEET POTATO & GREEN BEANS

Serves	4
Prep time	25m
Oven time	1h 30m
Total time	1h 55m

This is a simple, tasty treat any night of the week. pork belly is a relatively economic cut and a wholesome meal to make, but rest assured, it will be packed with real flavour. This recipe will not disappoint. I normally add green beans as a great side accompaniment, gently boiled for 10 minutes until tender and then drain and serve.

INGREDIENTS

- 8 slices of pork belly slices
- 1 tsp of olive oil
- 1 tsp of cayenne pepper
- 1 tsp of dried paprika
- Ground black pepper
- 1 tsp of dried oregano

- 1 tsp of dried thyme
- Rough ground sea salt
- 1 tbsp of soy sauce
- 1 Red bell pepper, diced into small chunks
- 1 tsp of fresh grated ginger

- 2 medium sized sweet potatoes cut into chunks
- A handful of green beans

METHOD

1. Pre-heat the oven to 220C (425F) ready for the pork. Combine the seasoning mix: cayenne pepper, dried paprika, pepper, salt, oregano, ginger and thyme together in a bowl with a tsp of olive oil. Now, brush the seasoning mix over all the pork belly slices and lay in a baking tray, set aside.

2. Place the tray of pork belly slices in the oven for 1½ hours until the pork is cooked to a light golden-brown colour.

3. Boil the sweet potatoes for 20 minutes, drain, add butter, ground pepper and then mash to a smooth consistency.

4. Boil the green beans for 10 minutes, drain, plate and serve with sweet potato mash and pork belly immediately.

VEG

Ultimate CRISPY ROAST POTATOES

Serves	4
Prep time	15m
Oven time	55m
Total time	1h 10m

Everybody who has ever had the pleasure to taste my roast potatoes, unanimously agree that they are the best they have tasted. These are truly the ultimate roast. Crispy golden brown on the outside and soft and tender on the inside. Once you've experienced these beauties, there is no going back.

INGREDIENTS

- 10 medium sized potatoes (Maris Piper or a waxy red)
- 6 tbsp of olive oil
- Rough grain sea salt

METHOD

1. Peel the potatoes and boil water in a pan on the hob. Once boiled, add the potatoes and par boil them for 10 minutes. It is important not to over boil at this stage otherwise they will just end up as mush.

2. Drain the potatoes in a cullender and toss gently, so all potatoes are fluffy. Half each medium size potato.

3. Then lay the potatoes on a chopping board and using a fork, gently ridge each face of the potatoes and then add to roasting pan. Continue with all potatoes.

4. Heat the oil in a rigid roasting tray on a heat of 220C (425F). Once the oil is sizzling, take out the roasting tray and place on hob. Now scoop up the hot oil and cover all faces of the potatoes.

5. Lightly sprinkle the rough grain sea salt over the potatoes and put in oven.

6. After 55 minutes or when golden brown, take out and serve immediately. If left too long, they will lose their crispiness and burn.

Classic
ROAST VEGETABLE BAKE

Serves	4
Prep time	15m
Oven time	45m
Total time	1h

This easy to prepare and cook accompaniment is always been a firm favourite with friends and family when paired with an appropriate main, such as Roast Chicken or lamb. It is so quick and easy to prepare and so rewarding to eat.

INGREDIENTS

- 4 tsp of olive oil
- 6 small parsnips
- 6 medium carrots
- 1 small swede – sliced in to thick wedges
- 1 red bell pepper
- Tbsp of fresh rosemary

METHOD

1. Heat your oven to 200C (400F).
2. Add 3 tbsp of oil into a roasting tin. Heat until you see the oil sizzling.
3. Now add the vegetables and roll them in the oil. Season with the ground black pepper, sea salt and fresh rosemary. Pour in the remaining oil.
4. Roast the vegetables for 45 minutes until golden brown and tender.
5. You can optionally brush with a thin coat of butter before serving.

Magnificent MUSHROOM, LEEK & SAGE PIE

Serves	6-8
Prep time	20m
Cook time	1h
Total time	1h 20m

The time taken to prepare and cook this amazing mouth-wateringly tasty pie is well worth the extra effort. The choice blend of flavours are not at all overpowered by one domant vegetable and this will be immediately apparent from your first bite. I hope you enjoy this scrumptious snack as much as I do.

INGREDIENTS

- 300g (12 oz) of mushrooms (mixed)
- 3 medium size leeks (or substitute with 25mm (1") of fresh ginger – grated).
- 3 sprigs of fresh thyme
- Olive oil
- 200ml (7oz) white wine

- 100ml (3½ oz) vegetable stock
- 1 tbsp of Dijon mustard
- 2 sprigs of fresh parsley
- 3 medium size eggs
- 180ml (¾ cup) of crème fraiche
- 25g (1oz) parmesan cheese

METHOD

1. Peel the mushrooms, wash and chop roughly. Pick the thyme leaves and then slice the leeks thinly.

2. On a high heat, place a large frying pan on the hob, add a few tbsp of oil, fry the mushrooms in several manageable batches and season with ground black pepper and salt. Fry until golden brown. Add more oil as needed.

3. When the mushrooms are cooked, set aside. Then put the frying pan back over the heat, adding 2 tbsp of oil. Now add the leeks and thyme. Cook and season over a moderate heat for 10 to 15 minutes, until the leeks are soft.

4. Now add the mushrooms back into the frying pan and pour in the vegetable stock and wine. Simmer until the wine has been almost reduced completely.

5. Add the mustard into the mushrooms, then pluck and add the parsley leaves, pour over crème fraiche and stir.

6. Remove the frying pan from the hob and leave to cool.

7. Preheat the oven to 200C (400F)

8. Place a non-stick baking sheet into a 30cm wide shallow baking tin. Trim sheet to suit. Place pastry sheet evenly into the tin, press into edges taking care not to puncture the pastry. Trim the pastry around the top edge of the shallow baking tin.

9. Now beat the eggs together in a mixing bowl and mix into the leek and mushroom mixture.

10. Spoon the mixture into the pastry lined pie dish, then thinly grate the parmesan cheese evenly over the pie.

11. Bake in the oven on a lower shelf for between 30 – 35 minutes, until a gorgeous golden brown.

12. Once the pie is thoroughly cooked, remove it from the oven and cool to room temperature. It is now ready to eat.

Delicious DUTCH OMELETTE

Serves | 4
Prep time | 30m
Cook time | 30m
Total time | 1h

I first came across this version of the ubiquitous omelette when I made my first visit to Holland at the tender age of 14 and it has been a firm favourite of mine ever since. It is a simple, but very tasty meal that has been passed down though the ages in Holland and can be found in most of the fine cafes and restaurants around the country. My first taste of a Dutch omelette was in the great river city of Nijmegen, close to Arnhem. Quick to prepare and simple to cook. I hope you enjoy this quick, tasty, nutritious meal as much as I do.

INGREDIENTS

- 2 tbsp of rapeseed or olive oil
- 350g (¾ lb) of new potatoes
- 7 medium sized eggs
- Handful of green beans, topped, tailed and rinsed

- 1 bunch of spring onions
- 1 pinch of freshly ground salt and black pepper
- ½ tsp of cayenne pepper
- 110g (¼ lb) of grated mature cheddar cheese

METHOD

1. Clean and cut potatoes into cubes. Place in a pan, cover with water, and bring to boil, then simmer on a lower heat for about 5 minutes.

2. Cut off the ends of the rinsed green beans and set aside then cut into roughly 3cm pieces. Now add to the potatoes and boil for a further 5-6 minutes on a medium heat. When cooked, drain veg really well and set aside.

3. Now lightly beat the eggs together, add cayenne pepper and season with salt and ground black pepper. Preheat the grill to medium-high heat.

4. Heat the oil in a medium sized non-stick frying pan over a medium heat. Add the spring onions and fry lightly for 4-5 minutes, until soft.

5. Add the potato and green beans and stir with the spring onions, making sure that all ingredients are scattered evenly around the pan.

6. Now pour in the beaten eggs. It's important NOT to move the egg around, just maintain a medium heat and let the mixture set slowly. After around 5 minutes, the top of the omelette will still be wet, but the base will be cooked.

7. Finally, sprinkle the grated cheese over the top, then put the omelette under the grill in the pan for 4-5 minutes. Cook thoroughly until golden brown on top.

8. Now place on a heat proof surface and cool for at least 10 minutes prior to slicing and serving. I never serve this meal hot from the pan. It is best served warm or cold.

Sizzling VEGETABLE STIR FRY

Serves	6
Prep time	20m
Wok time	10m
Total time	30m

This stir fry is so easy to prepare and really quick to cook, yet great on the eye and hugely nutritious and tasty. I always use fresh vegetables to prepare this colourful meal. You can also try with Pak choy, mushrooms, yellow squash and green beans.

INGREDIENTS

- 1 tbsp of olive oil
- 50mm (2") of fresh ginger, finely diced
- 4 peeled, medium size, diagonally sliced carrots
- 1 pinch of freshly ground black pepper
- Pinch of sea salt
- 6 broccoli florets
- 2 tsp of toasted sesame seed
- Handful of sugar snap peas or mange tout
- 1 red bell pepper, sliced in strips
- 3 tbsp of good quality soy sauce

METHOD

1. Heat the oil on medium to high heat in a large wok on the hob. Add the carrots, stir fry for about 2 minutes, then add the remaining vegetables and stir fry for about 5 to 6 minutes, or when the vegetables become tender.

2. Now add the soy sauce and ginger, stir fry until evenly blended, sprinkle with sesame seed and serve over a bed of cooked rice as an option.

A final thought...

"

Most dear actors, eat no onions nor garlic, for we are to utter sweet breath.

"

--- WILLIAM SHAKESPEARE, A MIDSUMMER NIGHT'S DREAM.

THE NO GARLIC COOKBOOK
Titles in the Series

Printed in Great Britain
by Amazon